THE IMPACT OF FAMILY VALUES ON LIFE STYLES.

Table of contents:

Chapter 1

Family living.

The family is the littlest and nearest unit in the public arena. The assets in the public arena like food, dress, cash, and asylum require sufficient administration. A family is a gathering of people or individuals who live respectively and are joined either by ropes of marriage, blood, reception or by birth and sharing of normal home. The family comprises of a dad and mother/moms and kids.

PREGNANCY: The period from origination to birth. After the egg is treated by a sperm and afterward embedded in the covering of the uterus, it forms into the placenta and undeveloped organism, and later into a hatchling. Pregnancy generally endures 40 weeks, starting from the principal day of the lady's last feminine period, and is partitioned into three trimesters, each enduring three months.

Pregnancy is the aftereffect of the preparation of the female ovum or egg by the male cell or sperm. Pregnancy is additionally the period from origination to birth. After the egg is prepared by a sperm and afterward embedded in the coating of the uterus, it forms into the placenta and undeveloped organism, and later into a hatchling. Pregnancy as a rule endures 40 weeks, starting from the primary day of the lady's last feminine period, and is separated into three trimesters, each enduring three months. Pregnancy is that state or condition when a female conveys an embryo in her belly for around nine months.

An embryo is an unborn child. The male sex cell is called Sperm. The female sex cell is called Ovum or Egg. It is created in the ovary. The method involved with creating an ovum by the ovary is called Ovulation. On the off chance that there is a sexual relationship or intercourse between a man and lady during the period the ovum is created, the sperm will treat the ovum, and this will bring about pregnancy. In the event that there is no sexual relationship during this period, the delivered ovum will cease to exist in a little while, then feminine cycle happens.

INDICATION OF PREGNANCY

Period stops

Bosoms become more full and delicate.
Areola become dim

Queasiness and spewing may happen, particularly toward the beginning of the day (morning disorder)

There might be successive pee

The midsection broadens from around 90 days

As the pregnancy progresses, the mother might feel the child's development

Delicate, enlarged bosom
Your bosoms might give perhaps the earliest side effect of pregnancy.

Weakness.

Slight draining or squeezing.

Queasiness regardless of retching.

Food revultions or desires.

Migraines.

Obstruction.

Mind-set swings.

Missed feminine period.

PHASE OF PREGNANCY DEVELOPMENTS

Pregnancy goes through three phases. Each stage requires 3 months. These stages are alluded to as Trimesters.

First Trimester: This is the initial three months of pregnancy. This is an exceptionally sensitive period since, in such a case that anything happens to the baby at this stage, it can prompt early termination or premature delivery. The placenta structures to give the embryo through the umbilical line.

Second Trimester: This is the pregnancy time frame somewhere in the range of 3 and a half year. This stage is more steady than the principal trimester.

Third Trimester: This is the pregnancy time frame from 6 to 9 months. It requires satisfactory sustenance for development. Toward the finish of this trimester, the mother goes in the process of childbirth and the youngster is conceived.

ANTENATAL: This is a clinical assessment a pregnant lady goes through during the time of her pregnancy before conveyance.

CHILD LAYETTE: A layette is an assortment of dress and frill for an infant youngster essential layette things frequently include:

a returning home-from-the-emergency clinic or birth focus outfit legless sleepwear (dozing outfits/kimonos/camping cots/infant sacques/cover sleepers) or footed sleepers

onesies (short-sleeved, legless bodysuits)/all-in-ones/rompers/coveralls undershirts/T-shirts

getting covers

wrapping up covers

hooded towels

child washcloths

fabric diapers for diapering

socks/booties

caps/beanies/sweaters/hitting (contingent upon the environment) burp fabrics (material diapers are frequently suggested)

Scratch gloves

Vests

Toy clatters/teethers/pacifiers

child bottles

Chapter 2

Human rights and violation

What Are Human Rights Violations?

The Universal Declaration of Human Rights (UDHR) was laid out in light of the monstrosities during WWII, including the Holocaust. The record frames the common liberties that all individuals are qualified for like independence from torment, opportunity of articulation, and the option to look for refuge. At the point when those freedoms aren't secured or explicitly ignored, they are disregarded. What are the kinds of basic freedoms infringement? Who is answerable for forestalling and tending to them?

Definition and kinds of common liberties infringement

A state commits common liberties infringement either straightforwardly or in a roundabout way. Infringement can either be purposefully performed by the state or come because of the state neglecting to forestall the infringement. At the point when a state participates in common freedoms infringement, different entertainers can be involved like police, judges, examiners, government authorities, and that's only the tip of the iceberg. The infringement can be truly rough, like police mercilessness, while privileges, for example, the right to a fair preliminary can likewise be disregarded, where no actual savagery is involved.

The second sort of infringement - disappointment by the state to safeguard - happens when there's a contention between people or gatherings inside a general public. Assuming the state doesn't do anything to mediate and safeguard weak individuals and gatherings, it's taking part in the infringement. In the United States, the state neglected to safeguard dark Americans when lynchings much of the time happened around the country. Since a significant number of those answerable for the lynchings were additionally state entertainers (like the police), this is an illustration of the two sorts of infringement happening simultaneously.

Instances of basic liberties infringement

We've referenced a couple of instances of basic liberties infringement, however there are some more. Common, political, financial, social, and social freedoms can be generally abused through different means. However every one of the freedoms cherished in the Universal Declaration of Human Rights and the legitimately restricting International Covenants of

Human Rights (ICCPR, CESCR) are viewed as fundamental, there are specific sorts of infringement we will generally consider more serious. Social liberties, which incorporate the right to life, wellbeing, and correspondence under the watchful eye of the law are thought of as by a larger number of people to be "original" freedoms. Political privileges, which incorporate the right to a fair preliminary and the option to cast a ballot, likewise fall under this classification.

Common and political privileges

Common and political privileges are disregarded through massacre, torment, and inconsistent capture. These infringement frequently occur during seasons of war, and when a basic freedoms infringement meets with the overstepping of regulations about outfitted struggle, it's known as an atrocity.

Struggle can likewise set off infringement of the right to opportunity of articulation and the right to serene gathering. States are typically liable for the infringement as they endeavor to keep up with control and push down insubordinate cultural powers. Stifling political privileges is a typical strategy for some legislatures during seasons of common distress.

Infringement of common and political basic liberties aren't generally connected to explicit struggles and can happen at some random time. Illegal exploitation is at present perhaps of the biggest issue on a worldwide scale as a great many everyone are constrained in the process of childbirth and sexual double-dealing. Strict separation is likewise extremely normal in many spots all over the planet. These infringement frequently happen in light of the fact that the state is neglecting to safeguard weak gatherings.

Monetary, social, and social freedoms

As portrayed in the UDHR, financial, social, and social privileges incorporate the option to work, the right to schooling, and the right to physical and emotional wellness. Just like with every single basic liberty, monetary, social, and social freedoms can be abused by states and different entertainers. The United Nations Office of the High Commissioner for Human Rights gives a small bunch of instances of how these privileges can be disregarded. They include:

Polluting water, for instance, with squander from State-possessed offices (the right to wellbeing)

Ousting individuals forcibly from their homes (the right to satisfactory lodging)

Refusing any assistance and data about wellbeing (the right to wellbeing)
Segregating at work in light of qualities like race, orientation, and sexual direction (The option to work)

Neglecting to give maternity leave (assurance of and help to the family)

Not paying an adequate the lowest pay permitted by law (privileges at work)

Isolating understudies in light of handicaps (the right to training)

Denying the utilization of minority/native dialects (the option to take part in social life)

Who is eventually liable for guaranteeing common freedoms infringement don't occur?

In common freedoms deals, states bear the essential weight of liability regarding securing and empowering basic liberties. At the point when an administration confirms a deal, they have a three-overlay commitment. They should regard, secure, and satisfy common liberties. At the point when infringement happen, government must intercede and arraign those mindfully.

This doesn't imply that individuals from common society don't likewise have an obligation to forestall basic liberties infringement. Organizations and establishments should conform to separation regulations and advance correspondence, while each individual ought to regard the freedoms of others. At the point when legislatures are disregarding common freedoms either straightforwardly or by implication, common society ought to consider them responsible and stand up. The worldwide local area likewise ought to screen legislatures and their histories with common liberties. Infringement happen constantly, yet they ought to continuously be called out.

Chapter 3

Family Conflicts And Family Crisis

Family conflict 3i

Any struggles that happen inside a family- - among married couples, guardians and youngsters, between kin, or with more distant families (grandparents, aunties, uncles, and so on.)

Kinds of Family Conflict

The contentions family middle people and advisors most frequently manage are: battling among married couples, kin competition, and parent-kid fights for control. As of late, numerous grown-up youngsters have been going to middle people to manage clashes connected with their older guardians. Arbiters can assist families with choosing living plans for their more established and frequently sickly guardians. They can likewise assist with questioning kin's choices on care-taking liabilities or how their folks' property is to be separated.

Dealing with Problems Destructively

Families caught in disastrous examples put the contention on individuals, rather than recognizing the genuine issue in question. They might demand that one party succeed to the detriment of the other, and they frequently attempt to overwhelm the other party utilizing control, dangers, trickiness, or brutality. Families in ceaseless clash communicate in unbendingly arranged designs and will generally have a similar discussion again and again, wasting their time rather than helpfully resolving their concerns.

Culture

Despite the fact that relatives may all reside in similar house, they might be coming from various societies. Contrasts, for example, orientation and age can cause conduct that appears to be unreasonable except if one grasps the thinking behind it. The contention among married couples might be filled by profoundly instilled orientation generalizations. Despite the fact that orientation culture is continually changing and shifts with people, a few essential contrasts among guys and females can raise struggle without any problem. Age is another component. Frequently, the age distinction among guardians and kids is sufficient to say that the two of them come from various societies. What a parent sees as a young person's defiant way of behaving might be her endeavor to squeeze into the way of life of her friends. It is imperative for outsiders managing family struggle to endeavor to figure out the family's way of life. Seemingly the family's absence of sound judgment to an outside intervener may basically be because of implicit social suspicions.

Dealing with Problems Constructively

Families who can deal with clashes usefully move from zeroing in on individuals to zero in on issues. They endeavor to address everyone's issues as opposed to requesting their own to the detriment of others. They then convey plainly and pay attention to one another. This might sound basic, however it is challenging so that relatives could see a drawn out struggle. Right now, they might require an outsider, for example, a specialist or a middle person to assist them with better dealing with their relational intricacies. Families are a framework; at the end of the day, they are more than the amount of their composite parts. In this way, a family struggle is seldom because of only one relative. It is possible the association between all the relatives that are heightening the contention. Along these lines, specialists attempt to zero in on process, rather than content. Rather than agonizing over information disclosed, they investigate the way things were expressed and by whom. Strangely, the abilities that specialists have mastered in managing obstinate family clashes are currently being applied to socio-political struggles.

Family crisis 3ii

An emergency is something that causes one to take a stab at an alternate and strange answer for the issue. Any breaking of family connections that force an emergency is something that causes one to take a stab at an alternate and uncommon answer for the issue. Any bursting of family connections that powers redesign of the family design comprises a family emergency as well as a danger to family solidarity.

Sorts of Family Crisis:

Family emergencies are arranged into two:

1. Loss of financial help, demise, extreme and delayed disease, mishaps

2. Emergency that include social marks of shame like chastity and significant social catastrophes like conflict, financial expansion, and sorrow. In the primary characterization, there are two subtypes in particular regular and expected emergency and the emergency emerging from a family struggle circumstance.

Normal and Expected Crisis:

These issues emerge day to day in all families differing in time and degree from one family to another. As they are normal, they are likewise anticipated. Among these, some are past the control of the relatives for instance war, passings, mishaps, ailment, joblessness, or underemployment. Every emergency includes comparing changes in the family. Destitution and disorder structure a horrible organization, each aiding the other to add to the tragedies of humanity.

Man can't work because of ailment. A significant piece of his pay is spent on the consideration and treatment of illness bringing about a decline in pay prompting the destitution state of the family. Also, destitution condition brings about ailment. One needs to buckle down with a lacking nutritious eating regimen because of less pay and experiences physiological and mental problems and becomes unequipped for accomplishing any work.

The monetary misfortune additionally happens on account of different sorts of mishaps like harming, singes, consumes, suffocating, street mishaps, and so on. In the event that the provider meets with a mishap and may kick the bucket or become impaired, it makes more issues in the family.

On the off chance that one individual from the family falls debilitated the job appointed to him should be done by others with the resulting general sharing of liabilities. Assuming the wiped out individual is an acquiring part monetary pressure has additionally to be borne by making elective courses of action.

Emergency Arising From Family Conflict Situations:

This kind of emergency includes liberation from over-assurance or reliance upon families, sensation of being undesirable and dismissed by the guardians and clashes with the family members and among family, an undesirable youngster in the family, unlawful fetus removal or dismissal after birth, extramarital issues, separation, and spouse or wife pestering bothering and whining emergency.

Emergency Involves Social Stigma:

It incorporates drunkards, jobless, wrongdoing, physical and mental weakening, early relationship, pregnancy of unmarried little girl, and presence of intellectually lacking or genuinely impaired kids in the family. Issues that start inside the family out of the relational relationship are known as intra-familial and issues that are past the control of the singular family because of financial downturn or different catastrophes are known as extra-familial emergencies and influence a few families simultaneously while the intra-familial influences the individuals from a specific family.

Reasons for Family Problems:

Deficient relational relationship, class enrollment pressures, monetary and different burdens, and social shame are the reasons for family emergency and includes a danger to the family association to its structure and construction.

Impact of Crisis:

Any emergency is a disaster for the family. All individuals are impacted all in all. It makes distress, outrage, or pain for relatives and they assume their part without excitement. An emergency meaningfully affects the family.

Smart preparation, forfeiting nature of relatives, family versatility, family mix, loving relations among relatives, great conjugal change among a couple, friendly parent-youngster connections, family counsel, sort of control in direction, cooperation of spouse in exercises outside the home and past effective involvement in the emergency are immeasurably significant variables in empowering families to conform to an emergency. The spouse should be intellectually ready to confront what is going on with mental fortitude. She needs to retain the shock emerging from such issues to take care of the relatives.

A greater part of family issues are not heavily influenced by the family. They should be persevered with tolerance. Insightful preparation, close to home development, and the capacity to acclimate to new conditions will assist with confronting what is happening strikingly. It's anything but an undertaking to be achieved by a solitary person. The entire family should be reset, as a co-employable undertaking with the witticism "Joined we stand and isolated us all fall.It incorporates heavy drinkers, jobless, misconduct, physical and mental decay, early relationship, pregnancy of unmarried little girl, and presence of intellectually lacking or truly debilitated youngsters in the family. Issues that begin inside the family out of the relational relationship are known as intra-familial and issues that are past the control of the singular family because of financial downturn or different catastrophes are known as extra-familial emergencies and influence a few families simultaneously while the intra-familial influences the individuals from a specific family.

Chapter 4

Family Conflicts And Crisis Resolution Strategies

Not to say what shouldn't need to be said, but rather there are a wide range of family clashes. Some are little contentions that everybody has with their friends and family occasionally. Others are conflicts that run further and frequently spin around at least one relatives' dissatisfaction with regards to the way of life or decisions of another.

Greater struggles emerge most frequently during times of progress or change. Normal models incorporate somebody moving in or out of the home, a marriage or separation, migrating, somebody setting off for college or choosing to leave it, work changes, the introduction of a child, a kid beginning a game or other extracurricular, a minor turning into a lawful grown-up, or a difficult disease or passing in the family. Be that as it may, any pressure makes tempers more limited and contentions almost certain.

Family clashes can be problematic to everybody's everyday life — even those not straightforwardly involved. Mind-set and execution at work, school, and different exercises endure. The pressure snowballs, which prompts an ever increasing number of issues between relatives.

Battles might permit put in an awful mood, outrage, hatred, and other pessimistic feelings to rot. Best case scenario, they can make enduring or even long-lasting harm connections while possibly not effectively settled.

An effective goal is one where all individuals included feeling like they've been heard, comprehended, and had their viewpoints regarded – regardless of whether they're not noticed. All gatherings perceive each other's interests, conciliatory sentiments are offered were called for, compromises are made where conceivable, and everybody deals with the truth.

It's more difficult than one might expect, however it must be finished. More minor contentions are obviously a lot simpler to wrap up than long haul ones and those connected with significant life matters. Family guiding might be required for the most serious or important struggles.

Be that as it may, here are a few general tips to help keep or restore the harmony in your home.

12 critical proposals for settling family debates

Quit talking out of frustration. at the point when emotions run wild, everybody ought to step back and set aside some margin to chill prior to proceeding with the discussion. Contending bitterly is rarely productive, and frequently prompts erupting.

Think about whether as an issue merits battling about. Frequently, in homes where there's pressure or irritating issues, any easily overlooked detail can transform into a victory. Try not to become involved with contentions over insignificant things.

Separate the individual from the issue. Attempt to take a gander at the core of the matter impartially and examine it, as opposed to making things individual.

Comprehend that the objective is to determine the contention satisfactorily — not to win the battle.

Try not to hinder during a conversation. Allow everybody to finish their contemplations and pay attention to them deferentially. Assuming you're interfered, smoothly remind your cherished one that you gave/will permit them to talk continuous.

Recollect that paying attention to somebody and recognizing their side doesn't rise to complying with them or buckling under them. It's basically a piece of being deferential and fair, and no obvious clash is at any point effectively settled without it.

Keep an even, quiet tone and utilize your indoor voice. Yelling simply raises everybody's feeling of anxiety and puts them on edge.

Nothing at any point gets settled when individuals are shouting at one another; all goals happen.It's a sufficient banality that you've likely heard it, yet it's still truly solid counsel: Use "I" proclamations rather than "you" explanations. While discussing yourself, you pass on to others how you feel. While discussing others, you sound accusatory and put them on edge.

Pose inquiries to be certain you grasp others' interests, complaints, thoughts, and perspectives. Allow them to ask you inquiries for a similar explanation and answer genuinely without getting guarded.

Oppose the motivation to drag other irrelevant, irritating issues or sentiments into the ongoing clash. Keep fixed regarding this situation within reach, or, in all likelihood things are probably going to get off theme and revert, as opposed to continue toward a goal.

Conceptualize arrangements together and find regions where compromises can be reached.

Affirm that everybody is sure about the arrangement when one is found and that they are happy with it. In the event that there's a past filled with arrangements not being adhered to, put down it so there's an account of it. You might in fact have everybody in question sign maybe it were an agreement.

www.ingramcontent.com/pod-product-compliance
Lightning Source LLC
LaVergne TN
LVHW052110160826
845678LV00015B/3474

* 9 7 9 8 8 4 4 4 1 4 8 3 1 *